SPIRITUAL AEROBICS

Spiritual Fitness
Through the Disciplined Life

Linda Schott

Christian Communications
P.O. Box 150
Nashville, TN 37202

SPIRITUAL AEROBICS

Published by Christian Communications
A division of the Gospel Advocate Co.
P.O. Box 150, Nashville, TN 37202

ISBN 0-89225-298-7

Preface

To the student:

Sometimes I gently chide my husband for preaching a sermon on personal shortcomings. He, in turn, reminds me that though he is a minister of God, he is not perfect. Through the efforts of study and prayer he is made stronger.

As I wrote this book, I realized that I, too, have weaknesses, and never have they been more evident than in the hours I spent poring over the pages of this manuscript. As I penned each word I was reminded of the times my life has been cluttered and disorganized—standing for nothing.

Spiritual Aerobics was born of a cry much like the one in Hosea 6:3: "Oh, that we might know the Lord!" Because of that desire, I have endeavored in every way to win a victory over an undisciplined life.

Hosea then continued, "Let us press on to know Him, and He will respond to us as surely as the coming of dawn." As each chapter was born, so was born in my life a new enthusiasm for the Lord—for His word and for time spent with Him in meditation and prayer. He responded to my efforts as "surely as the coming of dawn."

And He will respond to your efforts as well. I know with a certainty gleaned from experience that the Lord will meet you somewhere in the pages of this book as you attempt to enrich and deepen your relationship with Him.

Our struggle for a disciplined life will continue as long as we live on planet earth. But through our efforts to change we have taken a giant step toward easing our frustration of failure. When we fall, God will be there to pick us up, plant our feet in the right direction, and gently nudge us on to our final goal—a disciplined life in Christ Jesus.

Linda Schott

Introduction

On a cold winter's evening, there's something hypnotic and soothing about a crackling fire. But three hours later it's a different sight. To all appearances, the fire is dead. There's nothing on the hearth but ashes. No light. No smoke. No heat.

But look again! At the bottom of the cold embers are some living gleams. If stirred up, they could start a new fire!

Our Christian walk is like that. At times we feel cold, lifeless. The fire has gone out. Trials and stress have smothered the flame. But in each of us is an ember that could be fanned to re-ignite the flame.

That's what discipline is all about. It's not just for kids! Discipline is for any Christian who wants to reach below the surface and come to know Jesus Christ as a close, personal friend. Who wants to turn Christianity into fruit-bearing service and to experience joy—the icing on the cake! Who wants to stir the dead embers and relight the fire. Who wants Christianity to make a difference!

The world is starving for changed people. For people who reach below the surface. Have you ever liked a person on first contact, later to find that she is very shallow? Perhaps her conversation centers around designer clothes and trips abroad—or what's happening on the daily soap. When you try to discuss something deeper, she changes the subject. Her life seems trivial, purposeless.

That's what happens when we live Christianity on the surface. It doesn't change our lives. We don't grow spiritually. We awaken each morning without anticipation—merely plodding from one day to the next. *Something* is missing!

In a recent survey of a ladies' class, seventy-five percent answered "yes" to the question, "Do you feel that something is missing in your spiritual life?" Of those who answered in the affirmative only a few could identify the missing ingredient. They named discipline—to study, pray, meditate.

That's what this book is all about. It's about deeper, fuller living. A journey together into the Lord Jesus Christ. Discipline for me and for you.

Webster defines discipline as "training that develops self-confidence, self-control, character, orderliness and efficiency." It isn't surprising to learn that it comes from the word "discipline." To be a true disciple of Christ, we have to practice discipline!

When you think of the word "discipline," children probably come to mind. But the word covers a larger area. I think of all the projects I have left unfinished because I lack the discipline to see them through. It's easy to quit!

Look at the dieter. Does this sound familiar? . . .

This chocolate pie I made is too tempting. I can't bake something for my family and not eat it. That's expecting too much. I guess I'm just going to have to adjust to being fat. . . , I'm really tired of all this dieting. . . .

And I know you've heard this one . . .

> I keep intending to study my Bible every day. There's just not enough time! With football games, appointments, television, cooking, cleaning. . . , Maybe next year I'll do better. . . .

This is *my* personal stand-by . . .

> Writing a book is demanding. I think I'll put it away for now. . . .

So we rationalize and join the ranks of those who say, "I'm getting tired. I think I'll quit."

Write these words on your heart *now*—before you begin this study:

> ". . . Let us not lose heart . . . for in due time we shall reap if we do not grow weary" (Galatians 6:9).

A long time ago, in Bible times people were called to the disciplines of fasting, meditation, worship and celebration. It was a part of their culture. They did it on a daily basis. No one had to tell them how to go into a fast, or how to break it. They already knew!

We must learn that which was so easy for earlier cultures. It's an exciting journey. At the end of each lesson are thought-provoking questions for group sharing, or for individual meditation.

Because it has been proven that we retain a large portion of that which we write, there will be questions to answer. This section is entitled "Take Five," a term which comes from show business when the performers take a five-minute break for relaxation. We'll take our break for discipline. It will include scripture to ponder—and to share. A section entitled "Together" is filled with innovative group activities designed to s-t-r-e-t-c-h your mind and to draw you closer to each other. Because scripture memory is a part of self-discipline, passages to memorize are suggested in each lesson.

In "Plunging Deeper" we will set goals and search for methods to improve self-discipline.

For the journey you will need only your Bible, your class book and a notebook—or the personal spiritual journal you have purchased to accompany this study.

Our goal is transformation—from a surface, shallow Christian to one who can feel, hear, and see into the depths. From old, destructive habits to new, life-giving ones!

Our means of attaining that goal . . . discipline!

It's time to open the classroom door—together! Happy journey!

Contents

LESSON 1

Bible Study—A New Beginning

The whole world is on a physical fitness kick. On every street people—both young and old—are jogging. The media is filled with information on how to be fit. Even our foods are fortified with vitamins.

We're better off than our ancestors physically, at least. But what about spiritual fitness? Read what Paul had to say,

> "For bodily exercise profiteth little; but godliness is profitable unto all things, having promise of the life that now is, and of that which is to come" (1 Timothy 4:8).

In other words, what good is it if we are at the peak of physical fitness but never feed ourselves spiritually?

We need a spiritual diet—the main ingredient being the Word of God! As a matter of fact, we are too long after it!

> "As newborn babes, desire the sincere milk of the word, that ye may grow thereby" (1 Peter 2:2).

Obviously, we will remain spiritual dwarves without it. And who wants to be a dwarf—physically or spiritually?

Why Study the Bible?

Think about it . . . What other book took

2000 years to write
was written in 3 different languages
on three continents
by 37 authors
with 66 parts?!

Is it any wonder it's been called "the greatest book ever written?" It has changed lives, inspired art and poetry, offered hope and strength to the weak. It can change your life! But first you have to spend time with it, just like you would with your best friend. You can't know the author without reading his letters to you. Would you call someone your friend and never spend any time with them?

We study the Bible because *Jesus wants us to have the abundant life.* Not a life filled with material luxuries, but with joy and awareness of the Lord and His plan for our lives.

"I am come that you might have life, and have it more abundantly" (John 10:10).

Webster defines "abundant" as "more than sufficient; ample; rich." Jesus came to this world so our lives might be rich in the things that really matter—in spiritual health and well-being, in friends and loved ones, in fellowship with our brothers and sisters.

The Bible gives us emotional guidance. We, as women, often don't understand our complex emotional system. Women everywhere express frustration with emotional ups and downs, the tendency to weep over small things, jealousy, and that plague of all plagues, depression.

Through the study of Scripture, we can define our emotions and see them from God's viewpoint. We can rest assured that He understands the tears that often fall. Does it not say in the Psalms,

". . . put thou my tears into the bottle; are they not in thy book?"

We can understand anger—its right and its wrong use. We learn through study to mend quarrels "before the sun goes down." We learn not to judge, thereby avoiding hurt feelings and more tears. We learn to "bear one another's burdens," and to care for one another through both the good and the bad. What other book can we turn to for such guidance? What other writer can we trust?

The shelves of every bookstore and library are filled with self-help books. Many of them are excellent, but if we read every one of them, and leave out the most important Book, we will be spiritually malnourished!

The Bible tells us how to live like Jesus. The Bible is the mind of Christ. We see Him in every type of situation, responding always in love. Through accusations and hatred He remained calm. His life was free of many of the frustrations we face in a modern world, but He was faced with temptations. He always came out on top. We can look to His life for answers to any problem we might face.

The Bible gives us the knowledge to discern right from wrong. As children, we form our values based on parental and peer group instruction. How much better it would be to have values based on biblical principles! Often we depend on Bible School teachers to do that kind of teaching. The Bible teaches that the laws be "written on the gates and doorposts and bound to the wrists so they shall be as frontlets between your eyes" (Deuteronomy 11:18).

We turn to the Bible for answers to difficult situations. Have you ever been faced with a situation you didn't know how to handle? With your mate? With your children? With a friend? The easy answer is not always there, is it? Yet if we have a store of spiritual knowledge, gleaned from the Word, almost all of these situations become workable.

In a teenage Bible class, the students were faced with the following dilemma:

"A man's wife was dying of an incurable disease. Medicine prescribed for a cure cost $2000 a dose. It only cost the pharmacist $200 to buy and dispense it. Because he did not have the financial means to pay for it, the man broke into the pharmacy and stole the medicine."

Question: Was the man morally wrong for stealing under these circumstances?

The class was asked what they would do in a similar situation. They attacked the issue from every angle, and it was refreshing and reassuring to see many turn to the Scriptures for support of their opinion.

What if you were faced with a similar situation? Only a person with a confident and serene assurance of the will of God gleaned from many hours in His Word, could face such a trial and come out ahead.

The Bible is the source of final answers. Death has plagued mankind since Adam and Eve. Most of us fear it, yet if we have full knowledge of the Scriptures, we can ease our anxieties, and even look forward to a better day. I've always wondered how people who do not know the Lord could face death. Without God's promises concerning heaven, death would be terrible and lonely. Through study we find that death is not the end. Our purpose for living is to prepare for that special reward awaiting us. And the Bible is the only book that tells us how to claim that reward!

Bible study brings special rewards from God. James tells us that anyone who looks intently on the Word and lives by it will be blessed in what he does (James 1:25). Have you wondered why your life seems to be falling apart? Have you wondered why nothing seems to be going right? Pick up the Bible, dust it off, and dig in! Receive the abundant life promised in Scripture.

Only in the Word can we find the secrets to life. And yet we let the Bible sit on the corner table, gathering dust—and use it to hold mementoes and dried flowers.

It's like the little boy who said to his mom, "Mother, isn't this God's book?" "Yes," his mother answered. "Well, we'd better send it back to God, because we don't use it here."

As mothers, what more beautiful memory can we leave our children than the memory of us with the Book open, poring over the pages, discussing it, and pointing out important messages to them. How else can they know that it is an important book?

Finally, *we study the Bible because we are commanded to do so!*

"Study to show thyself approved unto God, a workman that needeth not to be ashamed, rightly dividing the word of truth" (2 Timothy 2:15).

God wants us to abide in, delight in, look intently at, meditate on, observe, and love His laws. In other words,

He wants us to study the Bible! Once you begin a meaningful study of God's word, you will never be satisfied with a casual reading of it. The more you study, the more you will know God, and the more exciting your personal study will become.

Someone describes packing his bag for a journey. Just before closing it, he observes a small corner not yet filled. He says,

> "Into this corner I put a guide-book, a lamp, a mirror, a microscope, a volume of choice poems, several well-written biographies, a package of old letters, a book of songs, a sharp sword, and a small library of more than sixty volumes; yet surprisingly enough, all these did not occupy a space of more than three inches long by two inches wide."

"But how did you do it?" he was asked.

"Well, it was all in the packing. I put in my Bible," he replied.

> taken from *Leaves of Gold*
> author unknown

Lesson 1

Take Five . . .

1 After reading the lesson, write down 5 reasons to study the Bible. Use your journal for this.
2 Fill in the blank, using Bible references.
   The Word of the Lord is
   a _burning fire_ Jeremiah 20:9
   a _hammer_ Jeremiah 23:29
   a _sword of the spirit_ Ephesians 6:17

16

a *lamp to our way* Psalms 119:105
a *purpose law of liberty* James 1:25 *be a doer*
as *washing of the water* Ephesians 5:26
as *nourishment* 1 Peter 2:2

3. If you were told that one year from today all Bibles would be confiscated and destroyed, what would you do to put the Word in your heart?
4. What is your definition of the abundant life?
5. What are the rewards of deep, disciplined Bible study?

Together . . .
1. Share with the group a situation in which knowledge of the Scriptures and the applications of its teaching made a difference.
2. To illustrate the above, role-play the following situations:

   You discover the baby-sitter has stolen money from your secret hiding place.
   You discover your best friend has been gossiping about you.

Plunging Deeper . . .
1. Choose a very short book of the Bible, such as 1 John. Each day, read it through once. In your journal, write ideas, thoughts, and understandings gleaned from your study.
2. To fight "procrastination, the enemy of discipline," choose one thing each day that you do not want to do or have put off doing. Write it down the night before and pray about it. Then, do it!

Bible Memory: Psalm 1 *Blessed is the man that walketh not in the counsel of the ungodly, nor standeth in the way of sinners, nor sitteth in the seat of the scornful.*

17

LESSON 2

What Happens When We Study?

It's not easy to change old habits! The older I get, the lazier I get! I've read many books on time management—but none slice through the lethargy I sometimes feel. One thing, however, that gives me the boost I need to climb out of those pits is to pick up the Bible and read and digest what it has to say. Once I have made the initial effort to change the habit of neglect, the next time it is easier, and soon I find myself eagerly anticipating my next study session.

Jesus said,

> "He that hath my commandments and keepeth them he it is that loveth me: and he that loveth me shall be loved of my Father, and I will love him, and will manifest myself to him" (John 14:21).

Where can I turn to find those commandments except the Bible? As I turn to the Word I begin to notice changes in my life.

I begin to grow

We need the Word in order to grow. "As newborn babes, desire the sincere milk of the word, that ye may grow . . ." (1 Peter 2:2). My babies had to have milk, or they wouldn't have grown into the fine teenagers I occasionally see flitting about my house. We must have the milk of the Word to grow spiritually. Jesus said,

"Man shall not live by bread alone, but by every word that proceedeth out of the mouth of God" (Matthew 4:4).

Christian growth is an exciting process. The changes are not dramatic or instantaneous, but subtle and silent, making themselves known in gentle whispering. You realize one day that you have more patience with your children. You don't mind baking that casserole for your sick neighbor. Your listening skills have improved, and people are seeking your counsel and prayers. They, too, have noticed the change. You're growing!

A cleansing takes place

"Now you are clean through the Word which I have spoken unto you" (John 15:3).

How evil this world is! Sin and corruption surround us. Our children are being fingerprinted and videoed. The message we send them is, "I'm doing this so I can identify you when you're dead." No doubt they see the world as a place to fear. We have all become suspicious, expecting evil at every turn.

And so we pray—for a change in society, a change that will bring people back to morality. But to change the world, we have to change hearts. That's the starting place. Evil thoughts and deeds come from evil hearts.

Often one of my children will say, "How can I keep from thinking bad thoughts?" There's an old saying "You can let the birds fly around your head, but you don't have to let them roost there." If you want to keep evil thoughts out of your heart, replace them with the Word of God. David did.

> "Thy word have I hid in my heart, that I might not sin against thee" (Psalm 119:11).

Learn to use scripture in your fight against Satan. It works!

I find delight in His word.

It lifts me up when I am down. It gives me hope and encouragement to face another day. The Psalmist said,

> ". . . He brought me out of a horrible pit, out of the miry clay, and set my feet upon a rock, and established my goings. And he hath put a new song in my mouth, even praise unto our God; many shall see it, and fear, and shall trust the Lord" (Psalm 40:2, 3).

The Word brings joy to my soul. It is the Lord Himself speaking to me.

> "These things have I spoken unto you, that my joy remain in you, and that your joy might be full" (John 15:11).

Often we search in vain for joy. We spend millions on entertainment and travel. Yet joy is still not complete. The missing ingredient? A deep, close, personal relationship with the Lord, brought about through study and prayer. Try it. See if you don't agree!

I become disciplined

As I become disciplined in one area of my life, it will carry over into another. Have you ever felt good about yourself when you accomplish a goal or purpose? You can feel the same way when you discipline yourself to study.

After several days, you will find yourself *wanting* to do more for the Lord. You will be hungering and thirsting after His word. The more you study, the more you will want to study.

I feel more secure talking to others about Jesus

It's more difficult to persuade someone to do something that you know nothing about! Many of us fear doing personal work because we are afraid we will be asked a question we can't answer. Bible study gives us the boldness we need to proclaim the Word. How else can we be ready to "give an answer to any that ask concerning the hope that is in you"?

Lesson 2

Take Five . . .

1. Re-state in your notebook the purpose of this study.
2. What is the means by which we transform our minds? (Romans 12:2).
3. Look up Mark 7:21-23. In your notebook make two columns, heading them "EVIL THOUGHTS" and "GOOD THOUGHTS." Copy the *evil* thoughts mentioned in the passage. Write the opposite, *pure* thought or deed in the other column.
4. The Bible mentions specific rewards of study. Read the Scripture, then write the reward.

   James 1:25 _____

   Psalm 1:2-6 _____

   Psalm 119:98 _____

Psalm 119:99 _____

Psalm 119:100 _____

5. List some changes that take place in your life as you study the Bible.

Together . . .
Share with one another your favorite Scripture. Relate what this passage means to you, and why it is your favorite.

Plunging Deeper . . .
Continue your study of the short book you started last week. Take some time in class to relate new understandings.

This week, find a person who is hurting. Send them a note of encouragement. Include an appropriate Scripture.

Bible Memory: John 15:11

LESSON 3

Study—A Primer

Any plant that survives one year at my house is a cause for celebration! It's not that I don't have a green thumb! It's just that *most* of the time I forget to water them! When I finally remember, they don't look too healthy. The soil is like sand, and the leaves are limp and dull.

Sometimes my Bible reading goes through a dry spell, too. I see the words on the page, but they don't excite me. They don't seem practical. They're like the soil—dry!

My study time needs to be freshened up—just like the plants. There are creative, innovative ways to approach Bible study. As you practice them, you will become more and more disciplined. Your spiritual growth will be phenomenal!

The following suggestions can help you "freshen up" your own Bible study time: Never, never begin a study time without prayer!

Ask the Lord to make His word sweet to your taste so you can delight in it. There are several things you need to mention in your prayers:

1. *Pray for cleansing.* It establishes a clear communication with God. Often in study a hidden sin is revealed.

"For the word of God is quick, and powerful, and sharper than any two-edged sword, piercing even to the dividing

23

asunder of soul and spirit, and of the joints and marrow, and is a discerner of the thoughts and intents of the heart" (Hebrews 4:12).

God uses His word to reveal secret sins of failures. When He does that, stop your study and pray for His forgiveness.

"If we confess our sins, He is faithful and just to forgive our sins, and to cleanse us from all unrighteousness" (1 John 1:9).

2. *Ask Him to remove any preconceptions* about the Scriptures you are studying. Perhaps you have heard or studied something that is not correct. When God removes these preconceptions, he reveals new insights.

3. *Ask God to be your teacher.* Jesus said that the Holy Spirit would "teach you all things" (John 14:26). Here is an appropriate prayer:

"Give me the spirit of wisdom and revelation as I study today. Open my eyes so I can understand what You are trying to tell me through your Word. I want to know the hope that comes through being your child, and the great riches that are mine as a Christian. Because I believe, show me the greatness of your power during this study time. Enlighten my eyes with your understanding" (Ephesians 1:17-19, paraphrased).

4. *Never forget your purpose* for study. Your life will change as you abide in His Word and apply the Scriptures to your life. Great blessings will be yours.

"If you abide in me, and my words abide in you, ye shall ask what ye will, and it shall be done unto you" (John 15:7).

How can you pass up such a glorious promise?!!

Be consistent.

Think of God's word as food for survival. You don't cook a big Sunday dinner, stuff yourself and then starve the rest of the week because it's too much trouble to prepare more food!

To grow as Christ would have us grow, we must make His word a part of us—on a daily basis. Naturally, there will be days you don't even want to open the Book. Satan doesn't want you to, either! On days like that, try to read at least five minutes. Pick a Psalm, or Proverb, or a short book. Remember, we're after *discipline* here! And discipline comes through practicing something consistently.

Be systematic.

Except on rare occasions, don't just pick a random verse or chapter. Don't snatch up the Bible in a free moment and frantically search for something to read. Develop a plan! God speaks to us when we deliberately take time, thought and preparation in study. Some ways of doing this are as follows:

1. *Choose a major book and read through it.* Not just once, but several times over a long period of time. Notice the structure and flow of the message. Are some parts difficult to understand?

Many times we are under pressure to read the Bible through in a year. We are even encouraged to do so from the pulpit. I would rather spend a year on one or two books, and understand them completely, than spend a year reading the entire Bible and understanding nothing! Yet, how many times have I made that famous New Year's

Resolution—"I will read through the Bible this year—from cover to cover." I set myself up for failure!

Be patient with yourself. Old habits die hard! Sometimes it is difficult to get yourself out of a non-learning pattern. Keep trying.

2. *Read a smaller book every day for a month.* Each time you read it, it becomes more a part of you—of your thought processes and your life. Verses spring from the pages. Some speak directly to you at this time in your life. Write down your observations. Slow down! We're not running a race—just growing!

3. *Find a specific time and place to study.* A place where you won't be interrupted. Is that possible with young children? There's always nap time—or after the children are in bed—or early in the morning. The rewards far outweigh the groans!

This time should be planned into your schedule. Take the telephone off the hook. If your children are old enough to understand, explain to them that this is your time with God. One mother lets her children know it's study time by lighting a candle beside her study table. She marvels at how quiet the house becomes!

Encourage your children to study their own Bibles. Buy them a Bible story book series, and while you are reading, they can study their own lessons and discuss it with your later. That's building beautiful, lasting memories!

Be sure to select the time of day when you are most alert. It should be the best time of day for you. Only you know when your mind is most eager for learning and exploration. Use that time!

4. *Read from different versions.* After you have read a book in the King James Version, switch to another. Try

a children's version. This is especially helpful for difficult passages.

5. *Use cassette tapes* of Scripture. Think of all the opportunities we have for listening! Do you drive a lot, or walk for exercise? Are you ever tied up in heavy traffic? Listen to Scripture as you travel. Listen while you clean house. Any Bible bookstore carries inexpensive audio tapes of the Bible.

6. *Visualize it.* Try to imagine the scene. Close your eyes and see life as it was in Bible times. Bible history books with illustrations help make the scriptures real.

Concentrate on geography as you read, using Bible atlases or maps. It's exciting to trace Paul's missionary journeys by following him on a map!

7. *Read aloud.* You can feel the power of the written word when you hear it read aloud. The Song of Solomon portrays love through its rich cadences. Paul's letters are filled with emotion. The power of Psalms is felt when vocalized. Remember, we retain more information when it comes through the audio message center of the brain.

8. *Expect a blessing* from God every time you study. Don't end your study until you receive one. Ask yourself what God is trying to say to you through this passage. Be like Jacob, who said, "I will not let Thee go except thou bless me" (Genesis 32:26).

9. *Put what you learn into practice.* Don't be like the person who looks into the mirror, sees a mess, then turns away and does nothing to correct it. When we study God's word, we see into ourselves. We become better people. Changes take place.

The Bible is God's voice to you. You must believe it, claim its promises, and obey its commands.

Suggested Bible Study Aids
Eerdmans Bible Handbook (Eerdmans)
Eerdmans Concise Bible Encyclopedia
New Bible Dictionary (Tyndale) contains extensive bibliographies
Zondervan Pictorial Bible Encyclopedia (Zondervan)
Cruden's Concordance
The Geography of the Bible (Harper and Row)
The MacMillan Bible Atlas (contains the best maps)

Lesson 3

Take Five . . .
1. Fill in the blanks.
    God uses His word in our lives in many ways:
    We are _____ by the word.
    1 Peter 2:2

    We are _____ by the word. John 15:3

    We _____ by the word.
    1 Peter 2:2

    We are _____ by the word.
    John 17:17

    We are _____ by the word.
    Ephesians 6:17

    We are _____ by the word.
    Acts 20:32

We are _____ by the word.
Psalm 119:105

2. In your journal, list all the hindrances you have encountered to effective Bible study.
3. What is *your* best time of day to study?
4. Take one chapter of the Bible an analyze it in the following way.

> Read it three or more times.
> Write a paraphrase or brief outline of what the chapter says.
> Write the theme or major message of the chapter.
> Write down your major conclusion of what the chapter says and how you can best apply it to your life.

5. The word *testament* means *covenant* or *contract*. What are the two covenants of the Bible? How do they differ?

Together . . .
Discuss Question 2 above with others in your class.

Plunging Deeper . . .
A vow is a special, binding agreement to carry out a particular act. Make a vow and write it in your journal. *I will spend at least five minutes a day in the Word for the next three months.* Don't let anything come between you and the vow to God.

Bible Memory: Hebrews 4:12

LESSON 4

Write It In Your Heart

Several weeks ago I went on a retreat with my teenagers. Saturday afternoon I had several uninterrupted hours, so a friend and I took a blanket and our Bibles and went to a nearby lake. We sat under huge oak trees splashed with colors of autumn. The air was still, filled with the sounds of the surrounding woods.

We had studied this lesson the previous week, and both of us had been memorizing Scriptures. That afternoon we shared them. I was proud of my friend as she quoted Isaiah 40:28-31 by memory. Then she moved on to Philippians 4:4-8. She was pleased with her accomplishment and had drawn great strength from the promise in Isaiah 40. At several difficult intervals during the week, she said those verses to herself and was comforted by the uplifting words.

Why memorize

What are some benefits of memorizing Scripture?

1. Your prayer life will be strengthened.
2. Your efforts at soul-winning are more fruitful.
3. People seek your counsel.
4. You become more observant.
5. Your outlook and attitude change.
6. Your faith is strengthened.

Scripture memory gives you a firm grasp on the Word. Solomon mentions writing the word on the "tablet of your heart" (Proverbs 7:3). He also advises keeping scriptures within you so "they might be ready on your lips" (Proverbs 22:18). David says that a young man can keep his life pure by treasuring God's word in his heart (Psalms 37:31, 119:9-11).

Almost everyone has tried to memorize Scripture. Most of us have not met our expectations. Some fail to see the value. Some have a mental block. Many believe they are too old. Nonsense! Psychologists all over the world agree that only a small portion of the brain's potential has been tapped—at any age!

Pick up your Bible right now, and turn to a section of Scripture that has spoken to you in the past. Memorize it. Don't try just a verse or two. Bite off the whole chunk! Usually a thought or message contains more than just a few verses.

How to memorize

Before you begin, pray that God will put the desire in your heart, for sincere motivation is the key to success.

The following suggestions might be helpful:

1. Just as in Bible study, your mind must be alert. Pick a time that is best for your life style.

2. Say the passage aloud as you memorize. Close your eyes and try to visualize it as it would look on paper.

3. Break it up into natural phrases as you learn it.

4. Don't forget the reference. Say it each time you repeat the passage.

5. Repetition is important. Say the passage many times the first day. Then review it once a day for approximately thirty days. This will cause you to *overlearn* it. After a

month, you will only need to review the passage once every two or three weeks.

A good review time is as you fall asleep. It's a sure cure for insomnia!

6. Write the passage. Involve all your senses.

7. Use the verse. It is not truly memorized until you *cannot* forget it. The goal of memory work is not simply to learn a passage—but to live with it until it becomes a part of you, affecting the way you think and act. Use it in conversation, teaching, correspondence, and everyday life.

No other practice or discipline is more rewarding than memorizing the Word of God. It's useful. It pays great dividends. It makes you feel good—about yourself. And we could all do with a bit of that!

So take the Bible down from the shelf. Dust it off. Then dust the cobwebs out of your "thinker," and get busy!

Paul's admonition,

"I can do all things through Christ who strengtheneth me" (Philippians 4:13), includes writing God's word in your heart.

Lesson 4

Take Five . . .
Take it easy this week. Instead of spending your time on questions, use it to memorize a favorite passage of Scripture.

Together . . .
During class period, have those who have memorized

passages say them to the class. Encourage one another. Enjoy the beautiful sound of someone saying Scripture by heart.

Plunging Deeper . . .
Copy the passage you have chosen to memorize on a 3 × 5 card. Put it in a prominent place where you will be sure to see it many times a day. Read it aloud every time you see it.
Find someone who can do calligraphy. Ask them to write your passage in script. Then frame it as a reminder of your achievement!

Bible Memory: Colossians 3:16

LESSON 5

Prayer Is . . .

Do you *really* believe God answers prayer? Or can you identify with the following situations?

> "The doctor says he'll only live three months. Why should I pray?"
> "There are billions of people in this world. Death, destruction, and famine are everywhere. God doesn't have time for me!"
> "God keeps telling me "no." I'm going to stop praying."

Many Christians face nagging doubts about prayer because they don't understand what prayer really is. We practice it regularly. We talk about it at church and read about it in Christian publications. But what is this thing called prayer?

Prayer is a spiritual exercise—another discipline. It's vital for growth. It's necessary for survival. The strongest Christian you know wouldn't be that way if she hadn't taken time to pray. She is just as busy as you are! But somewhere along the way she organized her priorities and put prayer at the top of the list. She has disciplined herself. Through thinking and planning, she has worked out a system—a time—and a place. She has claimed the promises and power of prayer.

Prayer is . . .

Hope McDonald, in her book *Discovering How to Pray,* says that prayer is:

". . . simply walking and talking with Jesus each day. It is sharing our life with Him. It is being confident that God knows the heartache and loneliness we may be experiencing at the moment. It is the assurance that God is aware of the cold knot of fear that can grip our heart when we see our children choosing to walk down the wrong path of life. Prayer is the certainty that Jesus stands at the graveside of our loved ones and weeps with us. It is the security that comes from knowing He hears our smallest whispered cry for help."

Prayer can be compared with the warm breeze that blows in autumn, taking the leaves off the trees and sending them spiraling to the ground. You can feel that breeze, but you can't see it. You can see the results of prayer in your life and the lives of others.

Prayer is deep, close communion with God. It is a "wish turned heavenward." It is bringing Christ close and becoming the channel through which His power flows. It is a way to do something for the One who has done so much for us.

There are many reasons for prayer:

1. *It helps us fight temptation.*

"There hath no temptation taken you but such as is common to man: but God is faithful, who will not suffer you to be tempted above that ye are able; but will with the temptation also make a way to escape, that ye may be able to bear it" (1 Corinthians 10:13).

There is an old saying that, "Satan trembles when He sees the weakest saint on his knees." We can bring our temptations to the Lord, and because He, too, has been tempted as we are, we can draw strength to resist.

2. *It helps us when we sin.* We all sin and have shortcomings, but when the flesh is weak and we are overcome, we have only to approach His throne in prayer and ask, and it will be forgiven. David offered a beautiful prayer of repentance (Psalm 51:1-3).

3. *It helps us make decisions.* The decisions a mother has to make every day are frightening! None should be made without first being brought to the Lord with a request for wisdom. Jesus did that before He chose His disciples. We should pray for His will to be made known to us.

4. *It fights sickness* (James 5:13-16).

5. *It gives us an opportunity to serve.* "Bear ye one another's burdens" takes on a new meaning as we bow in prayer for a loved one, or a friend, or even someone we've never met.

6. *It strengthens and comforts us* (Hebrews 4:15,16). We find in the Bible that God is with us in our troubles (Isaiah 41:10) and that He remembers all our tears (Psalm 56:8).

7. *It is a command.* "For men ought always to pray, lifting holy hands unto the Lord.

Kinds of prayer

There are two kinds of prayer:

1. *Short and brief.* "These are also called "arrow, dart, quick-thought.") If I see an accident, I immediately send up a prayer asking God to be with the victims. If two children in my classroom are arguing, I ask God to help them work it out. When I am in a difficult situation, I ask

Him to give me the wisdom to show His love through my actions.

Stonewall Jackson was a man of "arrow" prayers. He said,

> "I have so fixed the habit in my mind that I never raise a glass of water to my lips without asking God's blessing, never seal a letter without putting a word of prayer under the seal, never take a letter from the post without a brief sending of my thoughts heavenward . . ."

These short, brief prayers are important—but we can't live on them. We must also pray the prayer of

2. *Worship and intercession.* In this longer and deeper prayer, we praise and worship God. We intercede for others, bringing them and their needs before His throne.

Prayer can change lives. It builds character. It brings victory. Insecurity is replaced with deep peace. Selfishness is replaced with giving. Hatred is replaced with love.

Lesson 5

Take Five . . .
1. In the following Scriptures, you will find seven outstanding reasons for prayer. Write them in your notebook.

  1 Timothy 4:7 and 2 Peter 3:18
  Matthew 7:7-11
  Ephesians 6:18
  John 16:24
  Ephesians 6:11, 12 and 1 Peter 5:8, 9
  1 Timothy 2:4
2. Some spiritual giants in the Bible prayed diligently,

and their prayers were answered. The following is a list of their names. Opposite each name, write the result of the prayer.

Abraham _____

Elijah _____

Hannah _____

Jacob _____

The early church _____

3. Write your personal definition of prayer and the role it plays in your spiritual life.

4. Think about your prayers—their content, their frequency. Write some adjectives that describe them.

5. Write the names of people you know who have prayed for you throughout your life. How have their prayers changed your life?

Together . . .
Share one or more incidents in your life in which prayer made a difference. Perhaps it was in the illness and recovery of a loved one.

Plunging Deeper . . .
This week, keep a record of how many hours you watch television. On the same sheet in your notebook, record how many hours you spend in prayer.

Write down the *one single* thing that keeps you from effective prayer.

Bible Memory: Psalm 51:1-3, Ephesians 6:18

LESSON 6

Prayer Habits
Teach Us To Pray

There are many lessons to be learned in this school of prayer. Some you may already know—others can inspire you to better prayer habits. It never hurts to s-t-r-e-t-c-h our concepts and preconceptions about the right and wrong way to do things. If a new idea is presented here, don't close your mind to it without first giving it a try. When we are creative and innovative, it freshens our prayer lives and gives us a new outlook.

Time
As in study, there is no one particular time that suits every need. Your time will be determined by your own circumstances and preferences. It needs to be a time of quiet, preferably following your Bible study time. Don't just sandwich prayer between other activities. *Make* time for it. Often we are guilty of giving God the "leftovers!"

The most popular time for prayer is the evening. We can clean the slate, ask forgiveness, express thanksgiving, ask for protection, and bring special petitions before Him.

There are distinct disadvantages to this time of prayer. Exhaustion takes its toll, and we want to say, "I'll do it tomorrow." Satan might play a role in that! He weakens our resistance and we try to justify our delay by saying, "I'm so tired—I need my sleep!"

In order to fight fatigue, plan ahead. Make a prayer list. Assume a sitting or kneeling position. All these suggestions will help keep you alert.

Does God understand when we fall asleep? I think He does. He accepts our prayer in the spirit it is given.

I have a favorite evening prayer I discovered in a book of classic prayers. Robert Louis Stevenson wrote and read this prayer to his family the night of his sudden death.

Go with each of us to rest; if any awake, temper to them the dark hours of watching; and when the day returns to us, our sun and comforter, and calls us up with morning faces and with morning hearts, eager to labour, eager to be happy, if happiness should be our portion, and if the day be marked for sorrow, strong to endure it.

Others like to pray early in the morning, when quietness lies over the household. One saint of old stated that he had to see the face of God each morning before he could see the face of man.

One couple I know set the alarm for 5 a.m., get their morning coffee, make themselves comfortable in bed, and spend 30 minutes to an hour reading, studying, and praying. Their walk with the Lord is evident. Their time with Him is precious.

Last year, due to a move, I found myself commuting to my teaching job—45 minutes each way. It was a beautiful drive through the rolling hills of Tennessee—but not one I enjoyed. I prayed for strength to finish out the year and for wisdom to use my time in the car wisely. Then I began spending at least fifteen of those minutes, each way, communing with God. A drive once dreaded became a source of blessing!

Perhaps you can plan a special "retreat" for a few hours a month, to get away alone with God. There are beautiful parks in every city. Find a place where you feel safe and comfortable, take your Bible, and spend some special time with God.

No matter how busy you are, the best gift you can give yourself—the most worthwhile thing you can do—is to sit alone at the feet of Jesus. Not rushed but relaxed feeling the strength and peace that comes from being with Him, loving Him, and sharing your life with Him through prayer.

Place

At one end of my bedroom are two long windows that reach to the floor. In the daytime I can sit by the window and see the trees and woods across the street. In the evening, when all is dark, I can sit on the floor by that window and see the glittering stars of the universe, the moon gliding silently across the sky. It is there, by my window, that I place a soft pillow and make myself comfortable to talk to my Lord. It is a special place, and a special time for me.

You, too, can find such a place in your home. An abandoned corner, a sunny, cozy room—a deck or porch—any of these could be fitted for devotional time. And don't forget your bed. To kneel at the close of day and talk to your Father before you crawl into the cozy warmth of sleep is a more potent sleeping medication than any doctor can prescribe.

Perhaps there are some woods nearby. Pick a special

rock or log, or a big, shady tree to rest under. God often speaks to us in the quiet of nature—in its sights and smells.

Wherever you choose, it should be quiet. It should be a place where you can retreat every day to meet with your best friend. Use your creativity—make a place of prayer in your home.

Posture

A few decades ago, it wasn't unusual to find all the men on their knees during prayer in a worship service. I often saw Batsell Barrett Baxter drop to his knees during prayer in chapel service at David Lipscomb College. I was impressed—and almost envious.

But I can kneel in my own prayer time. There is no specific command about prayer posture. Several positions are mentioned in Scripture:

1. *Sitting.* This is our customary position in church and at home during prayer. Since this is the posture we assume for most activities, I question how much reverence it speaks of. However, we find David sitting to pray (2 Samuel 7:18).

2. *Standing.* In many congregations, the people rise for prayer. The entire body must co-operate to stand, so to some it symbolizes that the body, mind, and spirit are in worshipful attention. It can also symbolize an allegiance to God. We stand for the pledge. We stand for the singing of the national anthem. Yet we feel comfortable sitting or slouching in the presence of the Lord!

This was the typical Jewish posture for prayer (1 Samuel 1:26, Nehemiah 9:4, Mark 11:25).

3. *Kneeling.* A favorite posture of many in their private devotion, it speaks of awe, reverence, humility, and dependence on God. We have the example of Jesus in the

Garden of Gethsemane, where He knelt in anguish (Luke 22:41).

4. *Prostration.* Ezekiel fell on his face and beheld God's glory (Ezekiel 3:23, 9:8 and 11:13). Most reserve this position for times of extreme anguish of soul.

Our posture probably matters little to the Lord. But you should consider the possibilities. In worship service you are limited, but in private prayer, why not adopt a variety of positions? Each has its own significance and advantage, and you will become more attentive as you alternate between them. Whichever you choose, make sure it is not careless and slovenly, but speaks of your respect and reverence for the Lord.

Ingredients of Successful Prayer

1. *Pray in the name of Jesus.* When we ask in Christ's name, we know that our Father will hear our prayer and answer accordingly (John 14:13, 14 and 15:16).

2. *Pray in accordance with the will of God.* (1 John 5:14, 15). Perhaps I pray for a new job because the salary is higher. In my present position I have limitless opportunities to serve others. But my prayer is a selfish one, prayed for greedy motives. It is my will—not God's. Jesus prayed, "Not my will, but thine." Shall we not do the same?

3. *Pray in faith.* Jesus said that our prayers will be answered *if we have faith* (Matthew 21:21). Faith is the expectation that change will take place. As you pray, imagine the prayer as answered. If you are praying for a sick person, imagine that person as he or she will be when recovered—bright, cheerful, full of energy and well-being. This tool will help you truly believe that God answers prayer.

4. *Make sure your life is in touch with Jesus*—in every way. Search your heart and make sure your motives are pure (James 4:2, 3), confess all sin (1 John 1:8-10), and hold no malice toward anyone (Matthew 5:24). Ask God to reveal your weaknesses to you—to make you aware of them—and then get to work cleansing your life of their dead weight. Only then can you feel secure approaching God's throne—in faith.

5. *Be specific.* Don't utter vague prayers—"Be with all the poor and needy in the world." Pick one specific group of people or even better, one specific person. If you are praying for your child, pray for one particular aspect of his or her life.

6. *Be consistent.* Don't pray for a lost sinner three days one week and not again for three weeks! Prayer is a discipline, which means it has to be practiced on a regular basis. Make a commitment!

Lesson 6

Take Five . . .

1. Write the "extraordinary" place where the following Bible characters prayed.

Jacob _ladder_

Jonah _whale_

Peter _on the water_

Hagar _under the scrub_

Hezekiah _in bed_

David _up on the earth_

the penitent thief _the cross_

2. What are we told to "ask" of the Lord?
    1. Ask _rain - plants_ Zechariah 10:1

    2. Ask _all_ Matthew 7:7

    3. Ask _pray believing_ Matthew 21:22

    4. Ask _faith_ James 1:6

    5. Ask _what you want_ 1 Kings 3:5

    6. Ask _diligently_ Deuteronomy 13:14
3. List some of your favorite places to pray. Describe them in detail.
4. There are prayers that God *must* answer. What are they? Use your notebook.
    John 6:37 Prayers for _____.

    1 Thessalonians 4:3 Prayers for _____.

    Luke 11:13 Prayers for _Holy S_ _____.

    Revelation 22:20 Prayers for _come quickly_ _____.

Together . . .
Discuss hindrances to effective prayer.

Plunging Deeper . . .
This week, try to spend at least ten minutes each day with
God in prayer. Be ready to share your discoveries with the
class.

Bible Memory: 1 John 5:14, 15

THE DIFFERENCE

I got up early one morning
And rushed into the day;
I had so much to accomplish
I didn't take time to pray.

Problems just tumbling about **me,**
And heavier came each task;
"Why doesn't God help me?"
He answered, "You didn't ask."

I want to see joy and beauty—
But the day toiled on, gray and bleak;
I wondered why God didn't show me,
He said, "But you didn't seek."

I tried to come into God's presence,
I used all the keys at the lock.
God gently and lovingly chided:
"My child, you didn't knock."

I woke up early this morning
And paused before entering the day;
I had so much to accomplish
That I had to take time to pray.

Selected

LESSON 7

Prayer—A Ministry

Intercessory prayer is the noblest of all prayer. What a privilege to bring friends and loved ones and their needs to the throne of God! I can do it boldly (Hebrews 4:16). My prayer life is enriched when I pray for others. I approach the true meaning of prayer as I pray less for myself and more for others. It gives me a feeling of self-worth and a reason for living! It lifts me out of myself and my self-centeredness and blesses the one for whom I am praying.

One warning—never, never agree to pray for a person and not follow through. Ask God to guard you against such an empty promise. It is easy to say, "I will pray for you," but not easy to do so! For this reason, you should have a prayer notebook. When you receive a request for prayer, write it down. Transfer it to the notebook as soon as possible.

Even when you have not been approached by a person for prayer, you can know when to pray for that person. If you feel a deep, disturbing sense of compassion, use it as a sign to pray for them. Take them as a prayer project. Then stand back and watch the changes take place—in their life as well as your own!

Group Prayer

In our ladies' Bible Class, a prayer list is handed out each week with the names of those who have requested prayer, the ill, infirm, and shut-in. Periodically, we review those requests and note prayers which have been answered. A woman with deadly cancer is expected to die a slow and agonizing death. Her final days are relatively pain free, and her death is swift. A teen-ager who has left home, returns. A lovely girl has a serious auto accident and is expected to face massive plastic surgery on her face. She recovers with just a few scars. These are but a few examples of our success with group prayer.

We have our own personal rewards, for we have been drawn closer together and our faith has been strengthened as we see the power of united efforts. As extra reward, left-over prayer lists are placed in the lobby of the building. We know that others are joining us in prayer, for each week the pile disappears!

Praying for the sick

God doesn't want any of us to be sick. Jesus spent most of His ministry healing the sick. He heals a sick person through our prayers. Here are some suggestions:

1. Remember you are not the healer, God is.
2. Have more than one person praying. "For where two or more are gathered in my name, there am I."
3. Ask for wisdom to know *how* to pray for each person.

Often we shun the subject of healing through prayer, for fear of being misunderstood and mistaken for "faith healers." We can better understand the necessity of praying for the sick by considering the following situation. If you knew you had a serious health problem—possibly terminal—and were told that no one would be allowed to pray for you, you would lose all hope. Depression and despair would set it.

We all would choose never to suffer, but to suffer without the prayers of those who love us would be death itself.

Praying for your children

As I look back over my life, I can see that others have prayed for me—from my birth right up to the present—just as I have prayed for my own children. I have prayed that:

1. they would know a close, personal relationship with the Lord.
2. they would be protected from evil.
3. they would develop their talents for the glory of God.
4. they would develop compassion for others.
5. they would find Christian mates.
6. they would overcome any situations that might cause them difficulty or indecision.

At times during their lives I have kept a box with specific, detailed prayer requests for them—especially during times of sickness or trial. In order to train myself to be specific in my prayers for them, I draw one request each day, and concentrate on that request only, rather than praying generally for their well-being.

If I have to be in the car for a long period of time, I write that request on an index card and place it on the dashboard where I can be reminded of the need.

Praying for your family

As I pray each day, I ask God to bless our home, to rule over the hearts of those who live there, and to keep us safe. I am often reminded of the words to the song, "Bless This House":

"Bless this house, O Lord we pray,
Make it safe by night and day . . ."

A ministry for the elderly

Older Christians often feel unneeded, unloved, and unwanted. To make their lives a prayer ministry would bring a feeling of self-worth and usefulness. You don't have to leave the four walls of home to pray for others. You can pray from a bed or a wheelchair. The aged and infirm, God's "shut-in" saints, can reach so many. God needs them. They have great power through their prayers!

It takes courage to pray for another person. It takes time and effort and a sacrifice on your part. But as you do so, you will see changes in your life. James states:

"Can both fresh water and salt water flow from the same spring? Can a fig tree bear olives, or a grapevine bear figs? Neither can a salt spring produce fresh water" (James 3:11, 12, NIV).

Conflicting attitudes cannot live in a person at the same time. William Law said:

There is nothing that makes us love someone as praying for him, and when you can do this sincerely for anyone, you have fitted your soul for the performance of everything that is kind and civil toward him. Be daily on your knees in a solemn, deliberate performance of this devotion, praying for others in such form, with such length, importunity and earnestness as you use for yourself; and you will find all little, ill-natured passions die away, your heart will grow great and generous.

With intercessory prayer you can go into the White House, a foreign country, or a prison. God's unlimited power can be unleashed any place on earth—for the benefit of many people—through a simple prayer!

Lesson 7

Take Five . . .
1. What changes take place as we pray for others?
2. What are some advantages of group prayer?
3. What are some things we are to pray for?

1 Timothy 2:1 _for all men_

John 15:16 _for all things have fruit in the Father name_

Luke 10:2 _workers + harvest_

1 Timothy 2:2 _authority_

Ephesians 6:19 _make known the gospel for all_

1 John 1:9 _Confess our sins_ _made known_

James 5:16 _for healing_

4. Intercessory prayer brings us into _____
   (1 Peter 2:5, 9).
5. List five people for whom you need to pray on a regular basis.

Together . . .
Begin a prayer project. Have someone make out a prayer list each week, and hand it out to each member of the class. In several weeks, check up on the answers to your united prayers.

Plunging Deeper . . .
Pick out one particular person—perhaps a loved one. Make a list of their needs, both physical and emotional. Write each request on a separate slip of paper. Each day for the next month, draw out one request, and bring only that request before the Lord. Keep a record of changes in their life.
On a scale of one to ten, how strong is faith in God to answer each prayer?

Bible Memory: John 15:16, James 5:16

LESSON 8

The Secret Strength of Solitude

Have you ever wanted to scream, "Stop the world—I want to get off!" Would you like to dispose of your "to-do list" for just one day? Do you daydream about being alone on a desert island with no responsibilities? Are you easily irritated? Not sleeping well?

Perhaps you can understand what the writer of this poem was feeling when he wrote,

> The world is too much with us; late and soon,
> Getting and spending, we lay waste our powers.
> Little we see in nature that is ours;
> We have given our souls away, a sordid boon.

There is a secret strength in solitude. Unfortunately, it often takes a tragedy—the death of a loved one, a serious illness, or an injury—to make us stop and notice the frantic pace at which we live. Then we automatically seek the recreating stillness of solitude. We cancel or postpone commitments to spend time alone with God—to strengthen inner resources—to reflect and renew our relationship with Him.

The Bible is filled with stories of those who were victorious through solitude. Joshua, when defeat seemed inevitable, stood alone to pray and won a victory over five kings. When Elijah communed with God, God sent fire from the sky to convince Ahab that He truly was God. Jonah spent hours in the belly of a whale, and it enabled him to preach to the people of Ninevah.

Jesus Himself calls us to Solitude. Over and over in the Scripture we are told of times when He withdrew from the crowds to be alone. It was His daily strength. His disciples often accompanied Him on these journeys into solitude. Each time they grew a little. The hours they spent in the upper chambers with Jesus enabled them to save 3,000 lost souls on the day of Pentecost.

But, you say, how can a woman who is avalanched with the responsibilities of raising a family, being a good wife, and holding down a full-time job find time for solitude? How can you lay aside the clamor of the world, lift your eyes to God, and quiet your mind? I am reminded of a poem that says,

> I have a treasure which I prize
> It's like I cannot find;
> There's nothing like it on the earth—
> 'Tis this . . . a QUIET MIND!

To have that quiet mind, you need days of retirement, when you can shut out the noise and be alone with God. But just as in the other disciplines, you have to make time to "Be still, and know that I am God." To do that, you must:

Take "minute" breaks of solitude. Grab those loose, unattached moments and turn them into times to renew yourself and your relationship with God. For example:

Set your alarm ten minutes early. As you stretch and limber up those creaky joints, think about God. Praise

Him for a new day. Think of all the things for which you are thankful.

In traffic. Turn on a soothing tape and try to relax. Center your thoughts on good, positive things.

In nature. All of God's gifts of nature are given to us to enjoy. They are God's handiwork. Make friends with the animals, the birds, and the trees and plants. If you love God's creation, you learn from it. Open your eyes! Awaken your senses. Celebrate life!

In special times. The first snow of the season is usually a time of awe and wonder. Take a walk and listen to the hushed stillness. Write a poem about what you see and hear. How does the snow feel? Look up—the stars and moon are a beautiful display of God's handiwork. The first warmth of a sunny spring day brings a special sense of celebration. Take the time to enjoy all these special gifts.

Don't throw away these precious snatches of time! They are meant to be used to explore the inner secret of Christianity.

Every man or woman who accomplishes anything for Christ makes solitude a priority. David says, "My heart is fixed, O God, my heart is fixed" (Psalm 57:7). Meditation is the best way to fix your heart on God during solitude or quiet time.

What is meditation?

Unfortunately, we use the term meditation to refer to a far-out, weird type of transcending this time and place to communicate with inner voices. In some religions, emphasis is placed on meditation of this type. I prefer to think of it as a deep communion with God—a time when I can quiet all the battles of the mind and listen for new insights.

It is a concentrated effort to discipline thought on a particular subject or idea, preferably from Scripture. It should be broad enough to include imagination as we ponder His Word. It is a linking of His life with our own.

As you select a particular verse or passage to meditate on, the following suggestions may be helpful:

1. Think about *specific* words in the verse and ponder their meanings and implications. Pick out phrases and identify in your imagination how they apply to your own life.
2. Put the verse into your own words.
3. Compare it with other Scriptures.
4. Relate it to your own personal experiences or circumstances. For example, in the verse mentioned earlier—"Be still and know that I am God"—think of the ways in which you are successful in slowing down your life and thinking about God. List them. Then think of your failures in that area. Admit your weaknesses to God. Ask His help in organizing a quiet time for yourself.
5. Always conclude with prayer. Ask Him to help you put His message into practical application in your life.

"This book . . . shall not depart from your mouth, but you shall *meditate* on it day and night, so that you may be careful to do according to all that is written in it" (Joshua 1:8).

We must incorporate solitude into our daily activities. No discipline comes to us automatically. Invest time in quiet, simple thought. The fruit of your labors will be an increased awareness of God and His plan for your life.

Lesson 8

Take Five . . .
1. Write your own definition of solitude.
2. Write your personal definition of meditation. Does it differ from Biblical teaching?
3. List three times in the New Testament when Jesus took time to separate Himself from others to meditate and rest.
4. What is the difference between loneliness and solitude?
5. In what ways are the discipline of Silence and the discipline of Solitude similar? (You might want to save this question until Lesson 9 has been studied.)

Together . . .
Discuss some hindrances to practicing solitude.
Discuss common beliefs about meditation. How does the class feel about the practice of meditation? Discuss misconceptions in relation to Biblical teachings on the subject.

Plunging Deeper . . .
List specific times and places available in your search for solitude. Practice five minutes of solitude a day this week. Practice meditating on a different verse of Scripture each day. Use the method outlined in this lesson.

Bible Memory: Psalm 51:10-12, Joshua 1:8

LESSON 9

Silence

Perhaps there should be a beatitude that reads like this:

Blessed is the woman who knows when to speak and when to be silent.

Unfortunately, as women, many of us have been blessed with a loose tongue! If there is anything that needs to be said, you can count on us to say it—plus a little more!

Silence is a discipline. It's something we have to practice consciously. It is cultivated through prayer.

The book of Ecclesiastes says, "There is a time to keep silence and a time to speak" (Ecclesiastes 3:7). It takes freedom to be silent. Freedom from the need to justify our actions. Freedom from the need to be the center of attention.

Aren't there some women you would rather not be with because they demand your utmost attention all the time? At a gathering, they do all the talking. When you want to discuss a problem, they would rather talk about their own.

When silence is golden

James says the man who can bridle his tongue is a perfect man. Perhaps he should have changed "man" to "woman." It is our nature to want to *talk* through every situation. Yet there are many times when silence is appropriate.

1. When comforting the bereaved. We feel we have to offer empty phrases to fill the silence of grief. Just as effective is a gentle touch, a hug, a few simple words such as "I love you."

The story is told about a little girl who lost her favorite playmate to death. She immediately went to the home to comfort the sorrowing mother. When asked by her parents what she said, she replied, "Nothing. I just climbed up on her lap and cried with her."

2. When tempted to criticize. Impatient with the imperfections of others and our own insecurity causes us to be quick to judge—most often negatively. We are told to judge ourselves before we judge others. (Matthew 7.)

Great peace of mind comes from being silent when we're tempted to criticize. The one who speaks no evil of another can face everyone boldly certain that they have said nothing to bring another person down.

3. When called upon to listen. How blessed it is to seek counsel with a silent friend—one who knows how to listen with a sympathetic ear. A friend, a child, a co-workers, a neighbor, even a stranger often doesn't need the meaningless chatter of well-meaning Christians.

"To draw near to listen is better than to offer the sacrifice of fools" (Ecclesiastes 5:1).

Know when you are being called upon to listen. When my teenage daughter says, "Mom, let's go for a walk," I know she really means, "Mom, I need to talk to you."

A famous psychiatrist many years ago found out, to his amazement, that people, when allowed to talk, were able to gain new insights as they revealed their problems. Freud was a pretty smart man!

The woman who lives her life under the disciplines of silence is a woman who lives the verse, "A word fitly spoken is like apples of gold in vessels of silver" (Proverbs 25:11). If we speak when we should remain silent we have missed the mark!

Cultivating silence

How do we cultivate this great discipline of silence?

1. Pray for a gentle, quiet spirit. It is difficult to remain unruffled in stressful situations. If you see it as a personal weakness, ask God to put a bridle on your tongue so your words will be few and meaningful. Wouldn't you like to be known as a woman who says something valuable when she speaks?

2. Mean what you say. In the past lesson we learned to keep our word.

"It is better that you should not vow than that you should vow and not pay" (Ecclesiastes 5:5).

3. *Think* before you speak! Better known as "Bite your tongue." Set a goal each day never to speak in anger—then work through your goal hour by hour. Practice silence when someone else's feelings are at stake.

The following was written by Miss Mary Stewart of Washington, D.C., and has been adopted by many business and professional business women's organizations all over the United States, as their official prayer:

"Keep us, O God, from pettiness, let us be large in thought, in word, in deed.

"Let us be done with fault-finding and leave off self-seeking.

"May we put away all pretense and meet each other face to face—without self-pity, and without prejudice.

"May we never be hasty in judgment and always generous.

"Let us take time for all things; make us to grow calm, serene, and gentle.

"Teach us to put into action our better impulses, straight-forward and unafraid.

"Grant us to realize it is the little things that create differences, that in the big things of life we are as one.

"And may we strive to touch and know the great, common woman's heart of us all, and, O Lord, let us forget not TO BE KIND."

—Mary Stewart

4. Spend some time each day in silence. Turn off the TV or radio, sit down, and breathe in the tranquil sound of silence! Our minds are geared to run at full speed, with endless "mind-chatter." Focus on being silent—not only in tongue, but in heart. Become acquainted with yourself. You might discover some interesting things!

5. Try to live one day without words. You will become terribly frustrated, for you have learned to communicate only through words. Try to find other ways to relate to others.

"Be not rash with your mouth, not let your heart be hasty to utter a word before God, for God is in heaven, and you upon earth; therefore let your words be few" (Ecclesiastes 5:2).

Lesson 9

Take Five . . .
1. Proverbs 18:21 says that _____ and _____ are in the power of the tongue.
2. After looking at Proverbs 12:25, Proverbs 15:4, and Proverbs 16:24, name some adjectives that describe the tongue.
3. How does James compare the tongue to a fire in James 3:5, 6?
4. Name some particular circumstances in which you find it hard to hold your tongue.
5. What are some suitable and appropriate ways of conveying sympathy to others?

Together . . .
What are some positive ways we can use the tongue?
What are some of the motives behind faultfinding and unjust judging? How do we often justify this use of the tongue?

Plunging Deeper . . .
If you are artistic, make a poster illustrating one of the following verses. Display it in your classroom.
   James 3:5b, 6
   James 3:7, 8
Plan an evening alone with a friend or your husband. Make it an evening of shared silence . . . in front of a fire, reading, etc. Discover the joy of silent communication!

Bible Memory: Ecclesiastes 5:2

LESSON 10

Service

If our Creator desired, He could stretch forth His hands and encircle all His children at one time. Instead, He has chosen to use His servants on earth to touch other living souls. Our own hands are God's consecrated instruments of touch. He uses those who are nearby to give the touch of comfort to His children who are in pain, to encourage those in despair, to offer hope to the weary and depressed. He works through us to bring others to Him. Therefore, we are to serve in every aspect of our lives—where we live, work, worship, and contact people.

A great Christian woman is one who serves others. Jesus taught this principle when He washed the feet of His disciples (John 13). In doing so, He showed us that none is too high or too holy to perform lowly tasks. When we serve, we touch the lives of others and the light of Christ shines through.

Who are we to serve?

Family. God put helpless babies and aged parents into our families so the strong could bear the burdens of the weak. As we do so, we become spiritually mature.

As we look at the many responsibilities of today's Christian woman, it helps to change our perspective to one of servanthood. The women's rights movement tempts us to view motherhood as a burden. Christ wants us to look upon it as a privilege. When we approach each day with enthusiasm, as an opportunity for service, the endless tasks become bearable.

We can search for ways to serve those we love—to build them up, to encourage them, to enrich their lives and draw out their gifts. This can be done through both word and deed.

Christian brothers and sisters

"Be kindly affectioned one to another with brotherly love; in honour preferring one another . . ." (Romans 12:10)
". . . Distribute to the necessity of the saints . . ." (Romans 12:13).

Being a Christian does not shield us from pain and need. We are to meet the needs of those in our fellowship. We can give assistance in 1) psychological, 2) physical, 3) spiritual, and 4) financial matters (1 John 3:17,18).

The basis of our fellowship is our shared life in Christ. We should use the opportunities to serve, to mirror the qualities of Christ to one another.

Our neighbor. Our neighbor is anyone who crosses our path. It is anyone who needs our help.

Woodrow Wilson once stated,

No man ever came to the end of his life, and had time and a little space of calm from which to look back upon it, who did not know and acknowledge that it was what he had done unselfishly for others, and nothing else, that satisfied him and made him feel that he had played the man. And so we grow by having responsibility placed upon us, the burden of other people's business.

How do we serve?

Through words. People are hurting more deeply than we know. Every Christian is called upon to help ease those burdens. There are ways we can encourage one another through words.

1. *Be observant.* Look for and mention admirable qualities.

2. *Use correspondence.* A short note or card can lift spirits.

3. *Make phone call.* Tell someone you care.

Remember the famous verse in Proverbs, "For a word fitly spoken is like apples of gold in vessels of silver."

Through courtesy. A simple "Thank you" or "I'm sorry" can break down barriers to communication and open the door to greater things.

Through hospitality. The Greek word for hospitality means "affection to strangers." The writer of Hebrews tells us to "let brotherly love continue. Be not forgetful to entertain strangers; for thereby some have entertained angels unaware" (Hebrews 13:1,2). In today's society it is often impossible to be hospitable to strangers. But there are many opportunities to open our homes to others . . . our children's friends, neighbors, visiting evangelists, traveling chorus members—and never forget those who visit our worship services. We should practice hospitality "without grudging." It's a command that often slips into oblivion.

Through listening. Our egos make it difficult to be a good listener. We think faster than we listen, and we often are thinking, "What will I say next?" instead of focusing on what the other person is saying.

Listening takes practice and concentration. It is a form of communication that is often overlooked. It needs to be nurtured. It requires a sensitive ear, a ministry-motivated mind, and a loving heart.

Through sharing burdens. We are commanded to "bear one another's burdens." There are many ways to accomplish this. Become sensitive to the clues people give. When you walk into a party or class or arrive at work, seek out those persons who seem downcast. It could be posture or facial expression that alerts you. Let that person know you care.

In order to share others' burdens, we need to be

1. supportive
2. available
3. caring

Each day ask God to reveal to you those people who are suffering. Don't neglect your family, but spend some time with those who hurt. It re-energizes you and strengthens your own relationship with God.

Through prayer. In Scripture, Jesus doesn't say "Go ye, therefore, all ye with dynamic personalities, good looks, extroverts, talented, teachers, and Scripture memory buffs—go and make disciples, and the rest of you can just sit around and sing hymns."

He said, "Go ye therefore into all the world, preaching the gospel to every creature" (Mark 16:15). This is regardless of personality or gender.

As women, we tend to ignore this command. Because of our fear of usurping authority, we allow men to do the evangelizing and overlook the limitless opportunities we have to bring others to Christ.

Your life is a teaching tool by which others learn about Jesus. It reflects your values, your respect for the Lord, how you raise your children, and how you handle pain and suffering.

Evangelism is not just sharing the gospel with another. It is sharing a lifestyle with Christ at the center. Share Him with others by:

1. *Having Non-Christian friends.* We feel guilty when we are seen with a non-Christian. We *should* feel guilty when we don't have any friends who aren't Christian! What better way to teach a person than through a deep-rooted friendship!

2. *Having parties and get-togethers.* Include non-Christians. Help them get to know personally, through example, how great it is to be a Christian.

3. *Having a neighborhood Bible Study.* There are numerous books and guides to help you organize such a study. Check at your local bookstore.

Service means sacrifice—of time and possessions. It makes us emotionally vulnerable. But it is never wasted ". . . for you know that your labour is not in vain in the Lord" (1 Corinthians 15:58). Every act of service that we do in the Spirit of and for Jesus Christ counts for eternity . . . for

> There is a destiny that makes us brothers.
> None goes his way alone.
> All that we send into the lives of others
> Comes back into our own.
> (Author unknown)

The next time you find yourself in a situation in which the opportunity to serve is present realize that God has a purpose for placing you there. Perhaps He has planted you firmly in the midst of people who need your special loving touch.

God is working through each of us to glorify His name so others can say, as Job did: "The hand of God hath touched me" (Job 19:21).

> When all the waves of human fame, human applause, and human flattery have died away upon the sands of time, the tiny wave of love you started in some kind word, some loving ministry, will be rolling and breaking upon the shore of eternity. Every song that floats from your lips in the spirit of love; every word of comfort to the sorrowing; every loving warning and admonition to the wayward; every prayer that goes out of the love of your heart for a friend in need; every word of cheer and solace to the despondent one; every such deed of love, however insignificant it may seem to you, will meet you at the throne of reward, and go with you in your shining train of influence and love all through the countless millenniums of eternity.
>
> James McConkey

Lesson 10

Take Five . . .

1. A lifestyle of serving is supported in Scripture.

2 Corinthians 3:6a	"Who also hath made us _____ _____ of the new testament."
2 Corinthians 4:5b	". . . ourselves your _____ for Jesus' sake."

Matthew 23:11   "But he that is greatest
                       among you shall be your
                       _____."

2. According to Matthew 16:24, in order to serve we
   must:
   a. _____

   b. _____

   c. _____
3. What is the difference between self-righteous service
   and true service?
4. What is Christ's definition of hospitality according to
   Luke 14:12-14?
5. Name some famous women of the New Testament who
   pleased God through their service to others.

Together ...
1. What are some reasons (or excuses!) we give for not
   practicing hospitality?
2. Review briefly the different ways we are privileged to
   serve. Rate yourself on how well you measure up in
   each different area. Use the following scale: 5 is the
   best, 1 is the worst. Be honest!

Through words	1 2 3 4 5
Through courtesy	1 2 3 4 5
Through hospitality	1 2 3 4 5
Through listening	1 2 3 4 5
Through burden-sharing	1 2 3 4 5
Through prayer	1 2 3 4 5
Through evangelism	1 2 3 4 5

Plunging Deeper . . .
Pick out one area of service in which you feel yourself to
be weak. List one or two ways you can demonstrate this
service in the next week. Make it practical—and not too
complicated! Then go for it!

Bible Memory: Instead of Scripture, memorize the poem
on page 67, "There is a Destiny".

LESSON 11

Orderliness

Do you leave household tasks unfinished?
Do your clothes match?
Do you have unfinished projects lying around?
Can you see the top of your dresser?
Do you always lose things?
Are you late to appointments and meetings?
Are you punctual in answering mail?
Are you late paying bills each month?

Erma Bombeck says organization is hauling the garden hose in before winter! The Bible says "Do things decently and in order." The writer of Proverbs says,

> "I went by the field of the slothful, and by the vineyard of the man void of understanding. Lo, it was all grown over with thorns, and nettles had covered the face thereof, and the stone wall thereof was broken down. Then I saw, and considered it well. I looked upon it, and received instruction" (Proverbs 24:30-34).

So we begin our study of the neglected discipline—orderliness. Without it you will fail in other attempts to lead a disciplined life. Without ordering priorities and managing time, you lose control of your life. Leading a disciplined life with Christ at the center is much easier with orderliness as your partner. Otherwise you will burn excess energy and lose precious time.

We want to deny that we are responsible for our lives—for our successes and failures. We would like others to think we are perfect, that we have no needs. But just as an alcoholic must first admit that he is one before healing can take place, we must admit that our lives are disorganized before we can begin the monumental task of putting everything back in its proper place. The starting place for the journey is orderliness.

The Devil's Tool

The devil uses his favorite tool as a weapon against orderliness—procrastination! It's the Number 1 reason we fail to achieve a rich, fulfilling life.

We Procrastinate . . .
Doing good deeds
Doing unpleasant tasks
Saying "I love you" or "I'm sorry"
Showing appreciation

> Just Now
> Never mind about tomorrow—
> It always is today;
> Yesterday has vanished.
> Wherever, none may say.
> Each minute must be guarded—
> Made worth the while somehow;
> There are no other moments;
> It's always, Just Now.
> *Author Unknown*

Felix, the New Testament politician, was the star procrastinator of his time. He put off the most significant moment of his life.

"Go away for the present, and when I find time, I will summon you" (Acts 24:25).

Reasons for Procrastination	*How to Overcome*
Laziness	1. Reward yourself
	2. Think positively
	3. Pray
	4. Remember, "The soul of the sluggard desireth, and hath nothing; but the soul of the diligent shall be made fat" (Proverbs 13:4).
Fatigue	1. Improve posture
	2. Institute exercise program
	3. Improve outlook
	4. Lower sugar intake
	5. Relax
	6. Attempt regular movement in sedentary job
	7. Delegate responsibility
	8. Begin regular sleep habits
	9. Remember, "Nothing is so fatiguing as the eternal hanging on of an uncompleted task" (William James).
Time Pressure	1. Learn to say "no."
	2. Plan each day.
	3. List things to do.
	4. Put the worst things first!
	5. Do the worst things first!
	6. Set deadlines.
	7. Beware of interruptions.
Clutter	1. Have a place for everything.
	2. Delegate specific chores in order of importance.
	3. Focus on one task at a time.

Disorganization   1. List goals, long and short range
2. Use visible reminders (notes to yourself)

Mood-Swings   1. Get a physical check-up
2. Check hormone balance
3. Relax and make time for leisure

In order to do things "decently and in order," we must first look at each area of our lives, do some soul-searching and praying, and then start to work! Perhaps the following suggestions will help:

Putting Your Life in Order

1. *Money matters.* Many marriages fall apart because of unwise planning in the financial area of life. Some women are known for "impulse" spending. Some don't know *anything* about the family finances!

Money can be spent, saved, or invested. An honest look at your spending habits can be time well spent. In your evaluation, look for weak areas. Some suggestions for improvement might include:

Keep a written budget. Make it realistic.
Set financial objectives and goals.
Review your resources—investments, life insurance, etc.
Set up a record system for storing receipts, cancelled checks, tax records, etc.
Make out a will.

You will probably discover (if you didn't already know it) that you need to cut back in some areas. Perhaps it would help if you:

Keep lists of what everyone needs.

Barter—or trade—services with neighbors and friends.
Remove credit cards from your wallet.
Stay away from stores and malls except for necessities.
Shop by mail or from catalogs.
Budget your funds.

2. *Leisure.* Does it seem like you're working longer and harder, but the joy you seek is always out of reach? Are the words "play" and "rest" strangers to you? Do you feel guilty when you take a short "break" for relaxation? Maybe it would help if you would:

Let up on yourself. Everything you do doesn't *have* to be for a specific purpose. Do something for yourself!

Give *play* and *rest* proper dignity. In order to be all you can be for the Lord you need a proper balance of work and play. Let go of guilt when you are idle or find yourself having a good time!

Live for today. Don't continually postpone plans for a vacation or fun time. Don't waste today by waiting for a *better* time to enjoy your leisure.

3. *Self-control.* You can probably hear the moans and groans of your fellow classmates as you begin to talk about this one! It is a stranger to no one! In elementary school we begin to hear about this discipline—especially in areas of controlling the tongue. But what other areas need special attention?

Dieting. Blessed are you if over-weight is not a problem! If so, perhaps you can apply what you learn to improving the *quality* of what you eat.

As we get older, our bodies require less food to meet their demands. Yet we keep eating like we did when we were teens! Pushing the plate away and learning to say "no" to that enticing piece of cake becomes increasingly difficult. We keep right on eating, often to the point of gluttony! It might be well to consider the words of Solomon on the subject:

> "When thou sittest to eat . . . consider diligently what is before thee; and put a knife to thy throat, if thou be a man given to appetite" (Proverbs 23:1).

Our bodies are the temples of God. We should treat them with respect. Paul admonishes us:

> "Whether therefore ye eat, or drink, or whatsoever ye do, do all to the glory of God" (1 Corinthians 10:31).

Exercise. The key here is simply to do it!

It is a common fallacy that, in order to be fruitful, exercise must produce pain and perspiration. Studies have proven that exercise, in small, simple doses on a regular basis, is just as beneficial. For example, you could exercise while watching television, sitting at your desk, cleaning house, watching a ball game, or taking a shower! Check out some books from the public library and become aware of "isometric" exercises and their benefit. Find a sport you enjoy, and ask a friend to join you. Ask your husband to encourage you. Keep a record of your progress. Work at it—and be consistent.

These are some steps to keep you on track with dieting and exercise:

1. Admit your need.
2. State your goal in writing.
3. Set target dates.
4. Outline a plan—how will you reach a specific goal?
5. Reward yourself when you reach an intermediate goal.
6. Don't get discouraged!

You have a right to be proud when you set a diet or exercise goal and reach it, for "the desire accomplished is sweet to the soul" (Proverbs 13:19a).

The tongue. Controlling the tongue is an everyday effort. Some verses to ponder:

". . . He that shutteth his lips is esteemed a man of understanding" (Proverbs 17:28).

"Oh, that you should hold your peace, and it should be your wisdom" (Job 13:5).

Anger. Our society is rampant with tales of abused wives and children. If people responsible for those hideous crimes had learned to control their temper early in life, they wouldn't abuse those weaker than themselves. Let's look at some Scriptures on the subject:

"He that is slow to wrath is of great understanding; but he that is hasty of spirit exalteth folly" (Proverbs 14:29).

"Be ye angry and sin not; let not the sun go down on your wrath. Neither give place to the devil" (Ephesians 4:27,28).

It's a sad fact, but a true one, that even in the church of our Lord there are men and women who cannot control anger. A split church is the child of anger. So is a split marriage, or a split friendship. Tame this ugly member that dwells in you.

You are responsible for your life. Only you can change from a slovenly, disorganized woman to one who is on top of the world! Consistency is the key. Paul tells us to be

"*Steadfast, unmovable,* always abounding in the work of the Lord, forasmuch as ye know that your labor is not in vain in the Lord" (1 Corinthians 15:58).

It's not an easy journey—this road to becoming a disciplined woman. It will be marked with highs and lows. You will fail. You will want to give up. But keep that goal in front of you—to lead a disciplined life with Christ at the center. Whatever your weakness, recognize it and work on it. And most important—*stick to it!*

"Let us not be weary in well-doing: for in due season we shall reap, if we faint not" (Galatians 6:9).

Lesson 11

Take Five . . .

1. What does John 9:4 reveal to us about procrastination?
2. How is Jesus life an example of time management?
3. What are the two most "cluttered" areas of your home? How could you effectively cut down on that clutter?
4. The following is a list of Proverbs on financial management. Write the Proverb and the principle it suggests.

    Proverbs 10:15 _____

    11:4 _____

    14:20 _____

    14:31 _____

    22:2 _____

    23:5 _____

5. In Romans 13:7,8 what does Paul tell us about our financial responsibilities? Does this prohibit the use of credit?

Together . . .
Discuss the implications of the "supermom" syndrome in relation to time management.
What are some effective ways of teaching your children to control anger?
What are some occasions when anger could be good.
Discuss some implications of having overweight people employed in a place of business.

Plunging Deeper . . .
In writing, state your area of weakness from the lesson just studied. Analyze it. Why do you think you have fallen into the trap of overweight, etc.? Make a list of short-term and long-term goals to achieve improvement. Set a target date for each. Set up a reward system—such as a new dress when you lose ten pounds. Pray for strength!

Bible Memory: Proverbs 24:30-34.

LESSON 12

Celebration

Who enjoys being with a long-faced Christian? One who looks at life as an endurance course rather than a beautiful song! One who can't see, hear, smell, taste or feel the exhilarating joys of just being alive?

Our lives should be a continual celebration! Every day should be a day of praise, joy and thanksgiving. Isaiah the prophet said,

"O Lord, Thou art my God; I will exalt thee, I will praise thy name" (Isaiah 25:1)

Many Christians reserve joy and celebration for the good times of life. We often misinterpret the scripture which says, "The joy of the Lord is my strength" (Nehemiah 8:10). We think, "I will be joyful when I am strong." We put off joy until the time is right, rather than realizing that joy itself brings us strength. Joy and celebration should not depend on circumstances! There are times in life when we cannot be joyful, but to wait forever for the perfect time to celebrate is a grave mistake.

Joy is at the core of all the disciplines. Without it they become heavy tasks, laden with discouragement and despair. With it each discipline brings a sense of fulfillment, pleasure and satisfaction. We receive joy when we think of God—that He is the creator of all things, that His power is limitless and His mercy and love and goodness are unceasing.

How to Rejoice

"Rejoice in the Lord *always*, and again I say, Rejoice" (Philippians 4:4).

How can we bear the fruit of joy and celebrate life and its blessings?

1. *Dwell on the good and noble not the bad.* God didn't promise a carefree life. He reminds us that in the world there *will* be trouble (John 16:33). The reason we can remain joyful is His presence:

"When thou passeth through the waters, I will be with thee, and through the rivers, they shall not overflow thee: when thou walkest through the fire, thou shalt not be burned; neither shall the flame kindle upon thee. Fear not for I am with thee: I will bring thy seed from the east, and gather thee from the west" (Isaiah 43:2).

When we open our ears and hearts to these words, we can remain joyful even in the bad times.

2. *Fill your life with good, simple things.* A picnic in the woods, a family gathering—all are reason for celebration. They don't require hours of preparation, yet they form a bond that can hold friends and loved ones together for many years.

3. *Look for serendipitous events*—events that illuminate life and make us more loving, vital, joyful and compassionate. A serendipity stirs the heart and lifts us above the everyday, commonplace complacency of life. A sunset on a glimmering lake, the first snow of winter—the face

of a newborn child—these are but a few of the everyday occurrences that give significance to life and open it up to celebration.

4. *Nourish a sense of wonder.* Celebrate the joy that floods the heart in touching, tender moments. God gives us *all* things to enjoy (1 Timothy 6:17).

5. *Don't retreat from involvement with life.* When we become apathetic, we close our senses. We become deafened to the sound of God speaking in the thunder of a roaring sea. We no longer are stirred by the majesty of a snow-capped mountain against a winter sky.

Nourishing Joy

Nourishing the senses frees us to experience those things which transport us to the very presence of God. Ignoring them leaves us adrift, dazed and confused, running *from* life rather than *toward* it.

Joy births joy. Like a snowball picking up additional snow as it rolls across the ground or the infectious laughter in a roomful of teen-age girls!

Never forget the joy and celebration of being with loved ones on holidays, anniversaries, birthdays. If you can't find an occasion to celebrate, make one up! Keep your life full of joyous events, and you will find yourself celebrating your very existence.

Have you ever enrolled in the school of child-watching? Spend a few days observing the wondrous joy that spreads over the face of a child over things we regard as insignificant. That's what celebration is all about. To become as a little child again, undulled by routine, repetition, and familiarity. To enjoy the moments when everything suddenly become fresh and new and marvelous.

Joy and celebration are found in trust. When you surrender your life to God and trust His ability to meet your needs, you can live daily in joyous celebration. Then you will have the freedom to choose joy and celebration as a way of life!

Lesson 12

Take Five . . .

1. What is the difference between mere gladness and spiritual joy?
2. There is a strength that comes from joy. Fill in the blanks after reading the following Scriptures.

    1 Corinthians 10:13   The joy of the Lord is our strength in the face of _____.

    Psalm 40:8   The joy of the Lord is our strength for _____

    Hebrews 10:32-39   The joy of the Lord is our strength for _____

3. Write five things you can be joyful about.
4. In Proverbs 17:22 we are told that joy doeth good like a _____
5. What are some ways you can incorporate the discipline of joy and celebration into your family life?

Together . . .

Discuss the latest medical findings on the benefits of laughter and celebration.

Why do Christians often go around with long faces? Is it tradition, genuine unhappiness, or ignorance.

Plunging Deeper . . .
Write a love note to someone in your family and hide it where it will be found when they arise. Note the difference it makes in that person's day.
Try to find something in your yard or house that you've never noticed before!
Do one thing this week to celebrate life with your family.
Be ready to share during discussion time next week!

Bible Memory: Isaiah 43:2,5

LESSON 13

Discipline Equals Growth

You have come through twelve lessons and have experienced growth. Congratulations! Perhaps the changes in your life have been dramatic or instantaneous, or perhaps they slipped into your life with a gentle whisper. Maybe you have noticed that you are not the same person! Do you remember our definition of discipline?

"Training that develops self-confidence, self-control, character, orderliness and efficiency."

You have just completed the training course! You have just learned the stepping stones to a disciplined life with Christ at the center.

You have learned that Bible study helps us to know Jesus Christ and His will for our lives, and that a thoughtfully organized approach to study will succeed. You've learned first-hand the reward that comes from a prayerful, deep study of Scripture. You've increased the rewards of study with Scripture memorization. When you need a verse to apply to a certain situation, it's there, written on your heart!

In addition to study, you've learned to pray, and have seen the rewards of prayer in your life and the lives of others. You've discovered that a special time and a special place—both planned ahead—have freshened your prayer life and changed your outlook on many things. You've stopped giving God the left-overs of your time and effort.

With solitude, you have accomplished the goals of study and prayer. Just a few minutes a day spent alone with God have taught you the secret strength of solitude. And as you have studied and prayed alone, you have grown in wisdom and knowledge of God!

Solitude and silence are twin sisters. Without the comfort and familiarity of silence, you haven't experienced true solitude. Having mastered and enjoyed the strength of solitude, you will never feel threatened by silence. You now know that being "silent" is better. Gentleness and quietness, cultivated through silence and solitude, have enabled you to remain unruffled through trials and stress.

You've learned that serving others must become a disciplined way of life. Your service now brings joy. It has meant a sacrifice of time and material possessions, but your labor "has not been in vain."

And then there's the lesson you groaned and shed tears over—orderliness! But you changed some slovenly habits and became responsible for your own life. You learned that laziness breeds fatigue and a disorganized life style.

By now you are celebrating your new, disciplined life. The journey has been difficult. We've all stumbled along the way, but we had each other to cheer us to the goal. Celebration is no longer reserved just for the good times, for our newly developed sense of wonder helps us rejoice each day. It pulls all the other disciplines together and pumps energy and life into each one.

Having practiced and mastered these classical disciplines of the spiritual life, you can now walk with confidence, knowing that the Lord is your Guide. He reveals Himself in the little things of daily living, and desires only that we yield to His divine guidance.

It is only natural that, at times, we will fail and our goal will seem unattainable. It will help to look back and see the progress we have made. Evaluate yourself periodically. Certainly there is much left to conquer, for the disciplined life is a challenge. It's one that Paul accepted.

"Let us lay aside every weight, and the sin which doth so easily beset us, and let us run with patience the race that is set before us" (Hebrews 12:1).

He also said to:

"Press toward the mark for the prize of the high calling of God in Christ Jesus" (Philippians 3:14).

Lesson 13

Take Five . . .
1. Write in your own words the purpose of our study. What is the reason for pursuing discipline?
2. List the fruits of the Spirit named in Galatians 5. How can developing a disciplined life bring forth those fruits?
3. Read 1 Peter 1:16. What are some requirements for a "holy" life?
4. What are some ways in which Christian service might become a *bondage*?
5. Read Ephesians 4:22-24. Contrast the walk suitable for a Christian with the walk of an unbeliever.

Together . . .
Discuss what you did to celebrate life with your family last week.
Have each class member tell their strongest discipline—and their weakest.
How has this study changed your life?

Plunging Deeper . . .
For the next six months to a year, review each lesson in this book for one week. Do the activities in that section again. Continue to grow as you pursue the work of Discipline!

A Final Good-bye

The Irish Blessing

May the blessing of light be with
   you—
light outside and light within.

May sunlight shine upon you and
   warm your heart
'til it glows like a great peat fire
so that the stranger may come and
   warm himself by it.

May a blessed light shine out of your
   two eyes
like a candle set in two windows of
   a house,
bidding the wanderer to come in
   out of the storm.

May you ever give a kindly greeting to
   those whom you pass
as you go along the roads.

Discipline Equals Growth

May the blessing of rain—the sweet,
    soft rain—fall upon you
so that little flowers may spring up
    to shed their sweetness in the
    air.

May the blessings of the earth—the
    good, rich earth—be with you.

May the earth be soft under you when
    you rest upon it,
tired at the end of the day.

May earth rest easy over you when at
    the last you lie under it.

May earth rest so lightly over you that
    your spirit
may be out from under it quickly,
and up, and off,
and on its way to God.